THE PRESIDENT AND THE EXECUTIVE BRANCH:
HOW OUR NATION IS GOVERNED

d States Government

THE PRESIDENT AND THE EXECUTIVE BRANCH:
HOW OUR NATION IS GOVERNED

Mark Thorburn

Enslow Publishers, Inc.
40 Industrial Road
Box 398
Berkeley Heights, NJ 07922
USA
        http://www.enslow.com

Original edition published as *The Executive Branch: Leading the Nation,* in 2008.

Library of Congress Cataloging-in-Publication Data

Thorburn, Mark.
 The president and the executive branch : how our nation is governed / Mark Thorburn.
    p. cm.
 Includes bibliographical references and index.
 Summary: "Learn about how the President is elected, what the Presidential duties are, and who runs the nation if the President gets sick"—Provided by publisher.
 ISBN 978-0-7660-4063-2
    1. Presidents—United States—Juvenile literature. 2. Executive power—United States—Juvenile literature. I. Title.
 JK517.T48 2012
 352.230973—dc23
                                   2011028543

Future editions:
Paperback ISBN 978-1-4644-0174-9
ePUB ISBN 978-1-4645-1081-6
PDF ISBN 978-1-4646-1081-3

Printed in the United States of America.

032012 Lake Book Manufacturing, Inc., Melrose Park, IL

10 9 8 7 6 5 4 3 2 1

Photo Credits: Allyn Cox, p. 46; Copyrighted by the White House Historical Association, p. 40; © Corel Corporation, p. 7; © Enslow Publishers, Inc., pp. 6, 72; Fort Campbell Courier, p. 57; Library of Congress, pp. 8, 14, 17, 23, 29, 32–33, 40, 42, 60, 62, 76–77, 82, 84; National Archives, pp. 25, 43, 86; National Park Service, p. 8; Painting by Gilbert Stuart, p. 53.

Cover Photo: Matt Rourke/AP Images. Description: Onlookers flock to the National Mall in Washington, D.C., to observe Barack Obama's inauguration, January 20, 2009.

CONTENTS

EXECUTIVE BRANCH

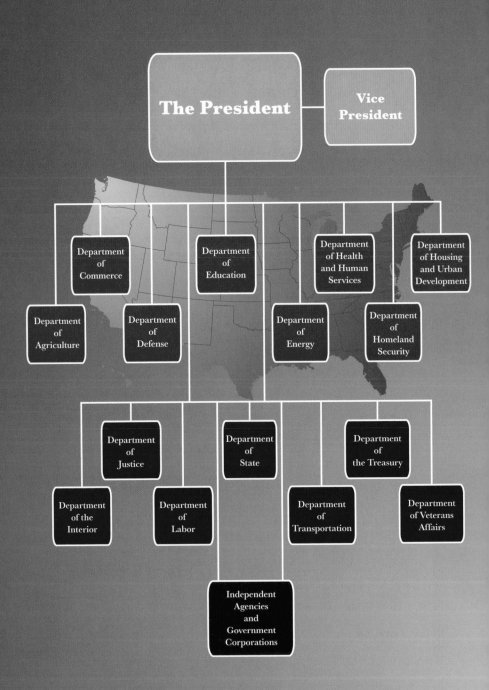

The President

Vice President

Department of Commerce

Department of Education

Department of Health and Human Services

Department of Housing and Urban Development

Department of Agriculture

Department of Defense

Department of Energy

Department of Homeland Security

Department of Justice

Department of State

Department of the Treasury

Department of the Interior

Department of Labor

Department of Transportation

Department of Veterans Affairs

Independent Agencies and Government Corporations

1

The Presidency in Action: The Cuban Missile Crisis

Twice in October 1962, millions of people around the world were glued to their radios and television sets. America and the Soviet Union were on the brink of nuclear war. Peace depended entirely on how Soviet leaders responded to a series of actions, demands, and proposals from President John F. Kennedy of the United States.

The threat began with the discovery of Soviet missiles on the island country of Cuba, just ninety miles off the Florida coast. But the main cause of the Cuban Missile Crisis was the rivalry between the United States and the Soviet Union. After World War II ended in 1945, the two countries were the only leaders on the globe. They became competitors in a contest to become the leader of the world. This rivalry was known as the Cold War.

One part of this competition was an arms race. The United States and the Soviet Union each tried to build more and more nuclear weapons. The leaders of both countries believed that they needed as many and as powerful weapons as possible in order to deter the other from attacking. The idea was that if both countries could destroy one another, they would never attack each other in the first place.[1]

Soviet leader Nikita Khrushchev (left) and U.S. President John F. Kennedy met in Vienna, Austria, in an effort to ease the tensions between the two countries.

Another thing that led to the Cuban Missile Crisis was the bad relationship between the United States and Cuba. In 1959, Fidel Castro took over Cuba. Ties between the two countries quickly turned sour. As this happened, Cuba established friendly relations with the Soviet Union.

In early 1961, the U.S. government attempted to overthrow Castro and his government by invading Cuba. However, this invasion, known as the Bay of Pigs, was a disaster and a major embarrassment for Kennedy and the American government.[2]

Two months after the Bay of Pigs incident, Kennedy met with Soviet leader Nikita Khrushchev in Vienna, Austria, to discuss several important issues. Very little was accomplished, and Khrushchev left Vienna with the impression that Kennedy was a weak leader. In turn, Kennedy thought Khrushchev was a bully. This, combined with the Bay of Pigs, made Kennedy and other American leaders want to appear tough every time they said or did anything about the Cubans or the Soviets.[3]

On October 14, 1962, the pilot of an American spy plane known as a U-2 took photographs of Soviet missile launching pads in Cuba. Next to the pads were Soviet long-range missiles that could be loaded with nuclear warheads. The pictures were shown to President Kennedy. The president immediately put together a group of special advisers called the Executive Committee of the National Security Council (or EXCOMM for short). For the next two weeks, President Kennedy and the EXCOMM discussed ways to respond to the missile threat. Kennedy and the committee also consulted with the heads of the army, navy, and air force as well as various diplomats and other experts.[4]

At first, Kennedy and the EXCOMM were in favor of bombing Cuba, but there was disagreement as to the extent of the attack. Some wanted to bomb only the missile sites, but others insisted on also bombing Cuban air defenses and any Cuban or Soviet bombers that might be found. This would reduce the risk of American planes being shot down during the attack and prevent a retaliatory strike against the United States. A few even wanted to invade Cuba. Then a member of the EXCOMM commented that sneak attacks by one country upon another were immoral and should not be done. It was also pointed out that, no matter what, it was impossible to destroy all of the Soviet missiles in Cuba. It would take only one of them to be launched at the United States for a nuclear war to start.

At this point, the EXCOMM discussed a new idea. President Kennedy could publicly announce the presence of the missiles in Cuba. He could then order a naval blockade of the island to prevent more Soviet missiles from arriving and demand that the Soviet Union remove the missiles that were already there. The term "blockade" would not be used because, under international law, a blockade was considered an act of war. Instead, the action would be called a "quarantine." To the members of the EXCOMM who still wanted to bomb Cuba, this action would serve as a warning to the Soviets. If Khrushchev did not remove the missiles within a few days, then the United States could still attack the missile sites and possibly invade Cuba. Others felt the demand could buy time to find a way to get the missiles out of Cuba without forcing the Soviets into a position where they might feel compelled to start a war.

On October 19, a vote was taken by the EXCOMM. By 12 to 5, it was recommended that President Kennedy blockade Cuba. Some, however, still wanted the president to order an immediate air strike. The EXCOMM then divided into two groups and, on October 20, each presented their arguments to the president. Kennedy decided to go along with the blockade.[5]

On October 22, President Kennedy shocked the world. In a televised seventeen-minute speech, he broke the news that Soviet missile sites had been discovered in Cuba. He tried to reassure the public that no nuclear warheads had been found on the island. Kennedy also announced plans to block all offensive military weapons that were headed to Cuba. Finally, the president made it clear that if the quarantine did not work, then further action (without saying what that action was) would be justified.[6]

The blockade was scheduled to begin on October 24. American warships surrounded Cuba to prevent any ship that contained missile equipment from reaching the island. In case the quarantine did not work or the Soviets decided to go to war, secret orders were issued for an invasion of Cuba. Troops were mobilized and nuclear missiles were readied to fire at the Soviet Union. Twelve submarines, each containing a dozen nuclear missiles, sped toward the Soviet coastline. Long-range bombers with a total of almost two hundred nuclear bombs were also put to flight. Other bombers with more than two thousand nuclear weapons were sent to military and civilian airports around the world. From these locations the bombers could attack the Soviet Union.

Twenty-seven Soviet cargo ships were in the Atlantic Ocean headed to Cuba on October 23. Nineteen of them were believed to carry military equipment, but no one knew what the vessels would do when they reached the quarantine zone the next day. To complicate matters, Soviet leader Khrushchev sent two contradictory messages. In one, he indicated that the Soviets would defy the blockade and continue sailing their ships to Cuba. But in the other, Khrushchev indicated that he was willing to negotiate in order to avoid a war. Furthermore, the Central Intelligence Agency (CIA) reported on October 23 that most of the missile launchpads in Cuba were complete and that the construction of the rest was speeding up. Also on October 23, an American U-2 spy plane was shot down and its pilot was killed while flying over Cuba, and another flying over the Soviet Union was almost intercepted by Soviet fighter planes.[7]

On October 24, tension was high as everyone waited to see what the Soviet ships would do when they approached the quarantine zone. To their relief, most of the ships hung a U-turn and went back to the Soviet Union. Of the few that continued on, all were stopped by the U.S. Navy. Then the Soviet ships were inspected to make sure that they did not carry any missile equipment before they were allowed to proceed. The quarantine worked. The problem now was to get out of Cuba the missiles that were already there.

The Soviets were outraged by Kennedy's action and demanded that the United States back off. In the meantime, construction of the missile launchers in Cuba continued. It soon appeared that the president would again have to face the question of whether to bomb or to invade Cuba. Then, on October 26, Khrushchev sent a personal message to Kennedy and offered to remove the missiles if U.S. officials promised never to try to invade Cuba again. That was followed the next day by a more formal letter in which Khrushchev said that the missiles would be dismantled if the United States withdrew its missiles from Turkey (an American ally that bordered the Soviet Union).[8]

Kennedy did not want to appear as though he was withdrawing the missiles from Turkey in order to get the Soviet missiles out of Cuba. Such a deal would make it seem like the United States was backing down under Soviet pressure. Kennedy was also afraid that the construction of the missile pads in Cuba would go on while the United States and the Soviet Union bargained back and forth.

President Kennedy and most of the EXCOMM now believed that war was again imminent. They decided that the United States could not risk nuclear war over a mere fifteen missiles in Turkey. But they needed to achieve peace without it looking like they struck a deal with the Soviet Union.[9]

Kennedy wrote a letter to Khrushchev on October 27 asking that construction of the missile bases in Cuba be halted, the missiles dismantled, and all missile equipment removed from Cuba. The United States would then end the quarantine and promise never to invade Cuba. The letter did not mention the missiles in Turkey. However, the president also sent his brother, Attorney General Robert Kennedy, to secretly meet with the Soviet ambassador to the United States, Anatoly Dobrynin.

The attorney general informed Dobrynin about the president's letter. He also said that it would soon be sent to Khrushchev and that its contents would be made public. This way the whole world would know what the United States was willing to do to peacefully end the crisis. Dobrynin was further told that America's military leaders were still pressing President Kennedy to invade Cuba (which they were) and that it was uncertain how much longer he could resist their demands. And Dobrynin was told that if the missiles were not removed from Cuba by the Soviets, then the United States would do it. Finally, as instructed by the president, Robert Kennedy offered a secret deal. The missiles in Turkey would be removed if the Soviet missiles in Cuba were withdrawn, but only if Khrushchev agreed that it was done at a later time and in such a way that no one would ever know that the two were connected to each other. Twenty minutes after the attorney general met with Dobrynin, President Kennedy's letter was broadcast by radio across the entire world.[10]

On the morning of October 28, nobody knew how the Soviets were going to respond. Everyone was worried about what would happen if they gave a negative reply. Then, at

Cuban leader Fidel Castro was not happy with Khrushchev's decision to remove the missiles from Cuba. This photograph of Castro was taken in 1959.

nine o'clock in the morning Washington time, a bulletin was read over the radio: Khrushchev had agreed to withdraw the missiles in exchange for a promise not to invade Cuba! Khrushchev also accepted the secret proposal from Robert Kennedy, but of course that was not revealed to the public.[11]

War had been avoided. President Kennedy was able to get the Soviet missiles out of Cuba while appearing to the world to have been tough with the Soviets. Khrushchev obtained the removal of the missiles in Turkey and a promise not to invade Cuba. Only Cuba's leader, Castro, was upset. He believed that he had been betrayed by the Soviets, but there was little that he could do about it.

2

Origins of the Presidency

A new constitution was written during the 1787 Constitutional Convention held in Philadelphia. The constitution that the United States already had, the Articles of Confederation, was not working well. One problem was that it did not provide for an executive branch of government to enforce the country's laws and to manage the affairs of the nation. So the delegates to the Constitutional Convention created a new office, the president of the United States.

The fifty-five men who attended the Constitutional Convention had many ideas about the presidency. They argued for months, but what everyone did not want was a repeat of what they experienced when America was part of the British Empire.

George III was the king of Great Britain when the United States declared its independence in 1776. He inherited his job from his father and held it for life. King George could not pass any laws by himself. But he could veto, or prevent the enactment of, any statute that the British Parliament adopted. The king also appointed the judges, generals, and other government officials who enforced the laws, fought the wars, and ran the government. And King George had other substantial powers that were limited only by the powers of Parliament. For example, he could declare war against a foreign country, but Parliament had to approve the spending of the money needed to fight it. Furthermore, in each of the thirteen colonies that later became part of the United

States, there was a governor appointed by King George who had many of the same powers. Over time, the Americans colonists perceived the king and his governors as tyrants who abused their powers.[1]

After independence, many states adopted constitutions that greatly limited the powers of their governors. For example, in most states, governors could not veto legislation nor make any appointments. In some, the governors had to share their few powers with a committee. Governors were often appointed by the state legislature, served in office for only very short periods of time (frequently for only one year), and could not seek reelection. But in contrast, America's new federal government did not even have an executive branch.[2]

Artist John Trumbull painted this representation of how things may have appeared at the signing of the Declaration of Independence. After breaking free from the British crown, the Founding Fathers were leery of having too much power rest in the hands of a chief executive.

★ Articles of Confederation

The Articles of Confederation were adopted shortly after independence was declared. Under that legal document, the United States was more of a loose alliance of thirteen independent countries than a single, unified nation. The president, who was appointed by Congress, was only Congress's presiding officer and had no power to enforce the laws of the United States or to do anything else that a king or governor could do. Indeed, no one in the federal government had those powers.

Besides not providing for an executive branch of government, the Articles of Confederation had many other problems. Once the American Revolution ended in 1781, the thirteen states started to fight among themselves. It did not take long before the United States faced disaster. So, in 1787, a group of delegates met to draft a new structure of government for the country.[3]

★ Constitutional Convention

At the Constitutional Convention, there were almost as many ideas about the presidency as there were delegates. One wanted a single individual with many powers, like a king, who would be chosen to serve for life. Others believed that the president should have very few powers and that the office should be held not by just one person but by a committee. Another group felt that the president should be required to share his powers with a council of judges.

How the president would be chosen was also debated. The length of the president's term of office was discussed, and many proposals ranging from three to twenty years were considered. There was also some argument as to whether the president should be able to seek reelection. And there was some question about who should have the power to remove the president from office, for what reasons, and how it was to be done.[4]

After four months of debate and compromise, the delegates to the Constitutional Convention decided, "The executive Power shall be vested in a President of the United States of America." In Article II, Section 1, of the U.S. Constitution the delegates set out the length of the president's term of office and the way elections were held. They agreed on the qualifications needed in order to become president and the method of selecting the president's successor. The powers, duties, and responsibilities of the president were listed in Sections 2 and 3 of Article II as well as in Section 7 of Article I. The method and reasons to remove the president were outlined in Section 3 of Article I and Section 4 of Article II.

3

Duties of the President

As the U.S.' chief executive, the president is responsible for the administration of the federal government. This includes the management of America's foreign policies and its relations with other countries, the execution and enforcement of the laws, and the carrying out of the government's programs. This job is obviously too great for any one person but involves thousands of government officials and employees who work both in the United States and around the world.

★ The President as an Administrator

To fulfill his responsibilities, the president is permitted by Article II, Section 3, of the Constitution to appoint ambassadors, judges, and other government officials to help him. However, to keep the president from picking only his friends and political supporters to fill these jobs, the Senate must approve many of the appointments. Senate confirmation, however, is needed only for jobs for which Congress determines the officeholder's length of time in office, salary, and duties. The president does not need Senate approval whenever he chooses someone for a specific but temporary job that Congress has not created. These include such tasks as representing the United States at an international peace conference or serving as a member of a presidential commission. Appointments to the Supreme Court and other federal courts also require Senate approval.[1]

Furthermore, the Constitution says that Congress can allow the president, the courts, and the heads of the various government agencies and departments to make appointments for "inferior offices" without first seeking Senate confirmation. Congress has, indeed, made such an allowance for most civilian government employees. These officers include the White House staff as well as the millions of government employees (such as secretaries and office assistants) for whom the president plays no role in hiring. Still, there are more than five thousand positions throughout the government for which the president must seek the Senate's approval before his appointees can start their jobs. The vast majority of these are routine appointments to jobs in such agencies as the Foreign Service, and fewer than a thousand every year take much of the Senate's time. There are also more than fifty thousand nominations within the military that the president makes every year that require Senate confirmation, but these are mostly routine commissions and promotions and very few need the Senate's full attention.[2]

★ Growth of the Government

When George Washington was elected president in 1789, there were only a few hundred "inferior officers" or federal government employees. However, that number has steadily grown. In 2006, there were over 3 million people (not counting the military) employed by the federal government.

Until the 1880s, most of these people received their jobs through the "patronage" system. This means that they got their positions either as favors from someone important in the government or as rewards for their service to the president's political party. However, public outrage at the abuses of the patronage system led to the adoption in 1883 of the first civil service law. These laws require most government employees to be selected because of their qualifications and ability rather than their personal or political connections. Today, more than 90 percent of the positions within the federal government fall under the civil service laws. Only the highest positions in the executive branch (most of which require Senate confirmation) can be filled by patronage.[3]

The president's ability to abuse his office is also limited by Congress's right to determine what a particular government agency or department can or cannot do. Congress also has the power to determine how much money each agency and department may spend and what the money is spent on.

Finally, the president's ability to manage the many agencies and departments of the federal government is limited by the immense size of the government. There are millions of employees and several layers of management are between the president and those employees who deal directly with the public. It could be months or even years before word of a new policy or a presidential order to change things takes effect.[4]

★ The President as a Law Enforcement Officer

The president is the chief law enforcement officer of the United States. It is his job to enforce the laws that are passed by Congress.

Congress does not have the right to make any laws that it wants. Instead, Article I, Section 8, of the Constitution has a long list of subjects that Congress can address. For example, it has the power to collect taxes, to maintain an army and a navy, and to regulate commerce between the states.

George Washington was elected to be the first president under the new Constitution. Previously, he had been the leader of the Continental Army during the Revolutionary War. This painting is artist Henry Mosler's impression of Washington as he crossed the Delaware River for the Battle of Trenton.

There are also other topics that Congress can pass laws on. For instance, the Fifteenth Amendment gives Congress the power to enforce the voting rights of Americans. But most importantly, Article I, Section 8, provides Congress with the power to "make all Laws which shall be necessary and proper for carrying into Execution the foregoing Powers, and all other Powers vested by this Constitution in the Government of the United States." In other words, if the ultimate goal is one that the Constitution permits Congress to seek (e.g., to maintain harmony between soldiers in the army), then any way chosen by Congress to achieve that purpose (e.g., the prohibition of racial discrimination in the army) is constitutional.[5]

Initially, the enforcement of federal laws was typically left to the local and state police, and the law enforcement activities of the federal government were limited to such things as collecting taxes. However, since the 1880s, Congress has passed a large number of laws to promote and to regulate the health, safety, and welfare of Americans. These laws cover many diverse subjects, such as the quality of food and drugs and the protection of the environment. As these laws have been adopted, more power and resources have been given to the president to enforce them. Most of today's 3 million civilian federal employees are involved in some way with the enforcement of federal laws.[6]

★ Enforcing the Law

The power of the president to enforce the laws is found in many parts of the Constitution. For example, he has the duty to "take Care that the Laws be faithfully executed." The president also appoints several government officials whose job it is to enforce the federal laws.

Among them are the attorney general, the U.S. attorneys, the director of the Federal Bureau of Investigation (FBI), and the federal judges. When necessary, the president can call out the military or the National Guard to restore order and to maintain peace.

Presidents have used the military on several occasions to enforce the law. The first time was in 1798, when President Washington used the army to stop a rebellion of farmers in western Pennsylvania who refused to pay a tax on whiskey.

President Gerald Ford pardoned former President Nixon for his role in the Watergate scandal on September 8, 1974.

Indeed, the entire Civil War was, technically, the use of the military by President Abraham Lincoln to enforce federal laws in the southern states.

The president's ability to enforce the law is not unlimited. Congress has the authority to stop him from enforcing a law by refusing to give him money to do the job. Congress can also restrict the president's ability to use the military for law-enforcement purposes.[7]

It was once argued by many that the president can enforce only the laws passed by Congress. But this argument was swept aside and the president's law enforcement abilities were greatly enlarged by two Supreme Court cases in the 1890s. First, the Court held that the president is empowered to enforce the Constitution and to maintain the peace within the country. Second, it was held that if anything interferes with the duties of the federal government, then so long as Congress has not already said what the president can and cannot do about it, the president can take any steps he feels are necessary to stop the interference. For example, when a violent railroad strike in Chicago in 1894 interfered with the government's delivery of the mail, President Grover Cleveland got a court order telling the strikers to stop their strike. He then sent in troops to enforce the order.[8]

★ Pardons

Related to the president's law-enforcement powers is his constitutional right to grant pardons and reprieves for crimes committed against the United States. A pardon is a total forgiveness for a crime or alleged crime. A reprieve is a reduction of a prison sentence or fine given by a court to a convicted criminal. The authors of the Constitution felt that this power would be more fairly used by the president than by Congress. The Founding Fathers were not only thinking about mercy; they also recognized that, on occasion, a pardon or a reprieve might calm the nation in troubled times. For example, President Gerald Ford pardoned former President Richard Nixon in 1974 for any crimes that Nixon might have committed during the Watergate scandal. Ford believed that to bring Nixon to trial would only delay the healing that the country needed after two years of political scandal at the highest levels.[9]

★ The President as a Legislative Leader

The authors of the Constitution believed that only Congress could ably represent the many different points of view that exist within the country. Therefore, the Founding Fathers gave Congress the sole power to make federal laws. However, the Constitution gives the president four ways to influence how those laws can be written.

The first way that a president can influence laws is to make suggestions to Congress for new laws that he feels are needed. The Constitution states that the president shall "from time to time give to the Congress Information of the State of the Union, and recommend to their Consideration such Measures as he shall judge necessary and expedient." This is the main tool that the presidents have to influence legislation and to pursue their goals for the country. Once an agenda is set, a president, directly or through his staff, his supporters in Congress, or the public, will try to convince the Senate and House of Representatives to adopt his proposals.

The country's first president, Washington, strongly believed that his main job was to enforce and not to make the laws. Therefore, he made few proposals to Congress. He also did little to persuade congressmen and senators to adopt his ideas when he did suggest them. Still, Washington indirectly pushed for laws that he was in favor of. He would send members of his Cabinet to Congress to seek the support of the legislators who would vote on the measures. The other early presidents followed this practice.[10]

★ Big Programs

The first president to propose a massive domestic program was John Quincy Adams, but Congress largely ignored him. His successor, Andrew Jackson, was the first president to appeal directly for public support in order to pressure Congress to adopt legislation. Jackson, however, actually had few new proposals and spent most of his time trying to stop the passage of laws that he disapproved of. The other presidents of the 1800s did little to try to influence Congress to enact new laws regarding domestic policy.[11]

The first modern president to take an active interest in the passage of legislation was Theodore Roosevelt. "Teddy" saw himself as the only public official who represented the entire country instead of local interests. He regarded his presidency as the sole avenue through which average Americans could get the laws they needed passed by Congress. Therefore, he frequently gave speeches to the public about his ideas and, with their support, pressured legislators to pass many far-reaching laws.

Roosevelt's successor, William Howard Taft, presented to Congress the drafts of proposed bills rather than just general ideas of what laws should be enacted. And the man who followed Taft, President Woodrow Wilson, actually participated in conferences held at the White House where bills were written for Congress to consider.

Theodore Roosevelt
Secretary of Navy, Rough Rider, Governor and President.
1858–1919
LITHOGRAPHED BY FORBES LITHO. MFG. CO. BOSTON~NO.12 FAMOUS AMERICAN SERIES.

Teddy Roosevelt often appealed to the public to gain support for his agenda and the laws he was backing. Perhaps that is why he was such a popular president.

★ Working With Congress

Every president since Theodore Roosevelt's cousin, Franklin D. Roosevelt, in the 1930s has initiated and guided his own legislative agenda through Congress. To assist in this task, President Dwight D. Eisenhower created the Office of Legislative Affairs and made it a part of the White House staff. The office informs the members of Congress of what bills the president supports and opposes. It also actively seeks congressional approval of laws that would implement the president's policies.

The president also works directly with Congress by meeting with congressional leaders and other members of the House of Representatives and Senate. Often, the vice president, the members of the president's Cabinet and White House staff, and other public officials are sent to Congress to push for certain policies. And the president frequently seeks public support for his proposals through speeches, press conferences, newspapers, and television. His hope is that the American people will pressure their senators and representatives to vote for the legislation the president wants passed.[12]

★ The Veto

The second way that the president can influence the making of laws is his use of, or his threat to use, his power of veto. A president vetoes, or prevents a bill adopted by Congress from becoming law, when he refuses to sign it. This way, the president can stop legislation that he does not like from becoming law. The mere threat of a veto often makes Congress give up on a bill or take out of the legislation the parts that the president dislikes.

The delegates to the Constitutional Convention distrusted an unrestrained legislature just as much as they did a strong presidency; both can lead to a dictatorship or tyranny. The Founding Fathers also believed that a presidential veto would help prevent the passage of bad laws. It was quickly agreed at the Constitutional Convention that the president should be able to veto legislation approved by Congress.

Some of the Founding Fathers wanted to give the president an absolute veto. That way, if he rejected a proposed law, Congress would have to rewrite the legislation to meet the president's objections or simply give up. But others felt that this would give the president too much power and allow him to stop the adoption of good laws simply because he disagreed with them. Therefore, the Constitutional Convention gave Congress the power to override a president's veto. It can turn the rejected legislation into a valid law by casting a two-thirds vote in both the House of Representatives and the Senate. In reality, presidential vetoes are rarely overridden. Of the more than twenty-five hundred laws that have been vetoed since Washington became president in 1789, little more than a hundred of them have been overridden.

The earliest presidents believed that Congress was the best branch of the federal government to understand what the people wanted. They also believed that the authors of the Constitution intended Congress to be supreme in making the laws of the United States. Therefore, they only vetoed bills passed by Congress when they believed the proposed laws violated the Constitution.

While in office, President Grover Cleveland was known for vetoing hundreds of bills that he did not feel were constitutional. This lithograph is from one of his campaign posters.

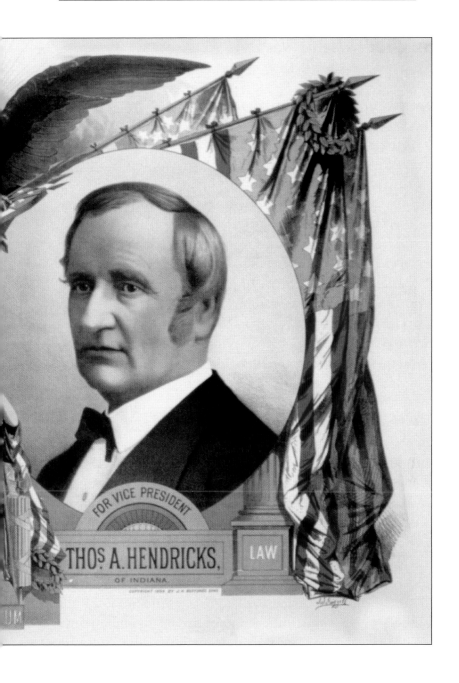

FOR VICE PRESIDENT

THOS A. HENDRICKS,
OF INDIANA.

LAW

★ A Wider Use of Veto

President Jackson rejected this idea. While Jackson was president, he and Congress often disagreed over what was needed to solve the country's problems. So, he used the veto to stop bills that he disapproved of. Jackson vetoed twelve bills, which was more than the combined number of the vetoes of all the presidents before him. This practice led many of Jackson's opponents to think of the president as a tyrant who was violating the intent of the Founding Fathers, and they called him "King Andrew the First."

President Cleveland also rejected the practice of vetoing bills only when he thought they were unconstitutional. While he was president, Cleveland strongly opposed the many bills passed by Congress that were written to pay excessive or phony claims to Civil War veterans. Therefore, during his two terms in office, Cleveland vetoed almost six hundred bills that were passed by Congress.

Aside from Jackson and Cleveland, most early presidents vetoed legislation only when they thought the proposed laws were unconstitutional. This still did not prevent bitter battles between the president and Congress over the use of the veto. This was especially true when John Tyler and Andrew Johnson were president. They believed many of the laws passed by Congress during their presidencies violated the Constitution. These fights led to attempts to remove both presidents from office by impeachment. Tyler was the first president to be the subject of a serious impeachment attempt. The attempt to get rid of Tyler in 1843 did not go far, but Johnson was actually impeached by the House of Representatives in 1868. He held on to his job by a margin of only one vote in the Senate.

★ Modern Veto Use

The first modern president to regularly use the threat of a veto to stop laws he did not like was Franklin D. Roosevelt. Every president since him has done the same thing. However, the frequency and the need to do so has varied depending on whether the House, Senate, or both were under the control of the president's political party. Typically, when they belong to the same party, members of Congress are less likely to pass laws they know the president will object to. However, when the majority of one or both houses of Congress are members of the opposing political party, they are less concerned with supporting the president. They will often have conflicting ideas as to how to solve the country's problems.

For example, two Democrats, John F. Kennedy and Lyndon B. Johnson, were president from 1961 to 1969. At that same time, the Democrats controlled both houses of Congress. During those eight years, Kennedy and Johnson vetoed fifty-one bills passed by Congress, and none of the vetoes were overridden.[13] But then two Republicans, Nixon and Ford, were president from 1969 to 1977. The Democrats still controlled Congress during those years. Together, Nixon and Ford vetoed 109 bills passed by Congress, and 19 of those vetoes were overridden.[14]

In the late 1990s, an experiment involving the president's veto power was briefly tried. When a president vetoes a bill, he rejects the entire piece of legislation. He cannot pick and choose the parts he likes and the parts he dislikes. Presidents for many years have asked Congress for the authority to veto parts of bills without rejecting the entire piece of legislation. Such a tool is called a line-item veto and, on the state level, many governors have it. The presidents claimed they needed it to cut wasteful government spending. Congress finally gave the president the power to use a line-item veto in 1996. However, the Supreme Court declared two years later that the veto violated the Constitution. While it was legal, President Bill Clinton used it to remove eighty-two items from eleven pieces of legislation.[15]

★ Impounding Funds

A tool that is similar to the veto, but not mentioned in the Constitution, is the president's impoundment of funds. Many presidents have impounded, or refused to spend, money that had been approved by Congress for specific projects. The money was often authorized by laws that the president had signed. The presidents who did this usually showed that the spending was no longer needed or that the project could be completed for less money. However, some presidents refused to spend the money because they disliked the programs the funds were meant for.

Nixon impounded more funds than any other president. For example, when Congress overrode Nixon's veto of an $18-billion bill to fight water pollution, the president simply refused to spend half of the money. Nixon also impounded billions authorized by Congress for other programs. The president claimed that he was trying to slow down inflation, but his opponents charged that he was really trying to undo Congress's spending decisions. Congress finally passed a law in 1974 (after overriding Nixon's veto of the law) that forbids impoundments unless they are approved by both the House of Representatives and the Senate.[16]

★ Two More Ways to Influence Congress

There are two other ways that a president can influence the making of laws. First and foremost, as the country's chief diplomat, the president can negotiate and sign treaties with other countries. These treaties become the law of the United States, but only after they are approved by a two-thirds vote of the Senate. Second, the president can convene a special session of Congress in times of national emergency. For example, President Franklin D. Roosevelt called for a special session of Congress in 1933 to deal with the economic crisis that resulted when thousands of banks across the United States closed during the Great Depression. However, such sessions of Congress are rare.[17]

4

Foreign Affairs, Vice Presidents, and Official Staff

The Constitution states that the president "shall be the commander in chief of the Army and Navy of the United States, and of the Militia of the several States, when called into actual service of the United States."

★ The President as Commander in Chief of the Military

The Founding Fathers were afraid that if they made an active military officer the commander in chief, then that person might abuse his authority, accumulate power, and become a dictator. By placing the ultimate command of the military with the president, the delegates to the Constitutional Convention sought to guarantee that America's military power would always remain under the control of the people.

Still, the authors of the Constitution were extremely fearful of putting too much military power in the hands of the president. Indeed, the Declaration of Independence is full of examples of how Britain's King George III abused his military authority. The Founding Fathers thus rejected this idea that, like King George, the president should have the sole power to declare war and to run the military. They were originally going to leave all war-making powers with Congress. But soon they realized that it would be too large to make certain wartime decisions, especially in times of an emergency. As a compromise, while the president was given the command of the U.S. military forces, a long list of war-related powers were left with the Congress. These powers include the ability to declare war and the authority to raise, to equip, and to organize the military.[1]

★ Authority of Commander in Chief

The president's authority as commander in chief is vague in some areas. The president can clearly defend the United States if it is invaded, as well as lead the country's military forces when Congress declares war. But the Constitution is silent about such issues as whether the president, without congressional authorization, can send troops into a fight if war has not yet been declared. These are not minor questions. The United States has fought only five declared wars (the War of 1812, the Mexican-American War, the Spanish-American War, World War I, and World War II) but has been engaged in several undeclared wars, including Korea, Vietnam, and Iraq. There have been more than one hundred additional military operations, many of which cost American lives and were not authorized by Congress.

★ Powers of Commander in Chief

After the adoption of the Constitution, most people agreed that the president could not engage America's military in any significant action without Congress's prior approval unless the United States was invaded. For example, when

President Franklin Delano Roosevelt signs the declaration of war against Japan, which brought the United States into World War II.

French privateers attacked American merchant ships, President John Adams went to Congress in 1798 for permission to fight back. Most people also agreed that once war was declared, the president's role was only that of acting as America's highest general and admiral. His wartime powers did not go much beyond directing the operations of the military. But it did not take long before the presidents expanded their interpretation of their powers as commander in chief.[2]

★ Expanding Powers of Commander in Chief

For example, after the War of 1812, Seminole Indians and runaway slaves in the Spanish colony of Florida frequently crossed the border to attack and to kill settlers in southern Georgia. President James Monroe, without congressional approval, secretly ordered the army to enter Florida, to deal with the raiders, and to attack any Spanish forts that were giving the Seminoles and the slaves aid and shelter.[3]

The first major expansion of the president's powers as commander in chief occurred during the Civil War. After the war began in 1861, President Abraham Lincoln was afraid that many in Congress would object to the measures that he thought were necessary to end the South's rebellion and to save the country. These actions included enlarging the army and navy, blockading southern ports, and authorizing the military to arrest and to detain civilians who were suspected of disloyalty. Neither the Constitution nor any law passed by Congress said that Lincoln could do these things. Therefore, he did not convene Congress for two months and, as commander in chief, took those steps without seeking its prior consent. Lincoln's actions were popular with the people in the North, and when Congress to met, it approved his decisions.

During the Civil War, Abraham Lincoln expanded the role of the president as commander in chief by making some military decisions without consulting Congress.

Later on during the war, Lincoln took more steps as commander in chief without first consulting Congress. These included ordering a draft to increase the size of the army, permitting civilians who were suspected of disloyalty to be tried in military courts, and freeing the slaves in the Confederacy (which at the time deprived slave owners of their lawful private property without a court hearing or compensation). Lincoln knew that some of his actions violated the Constitution but said it was better to do that and keep the United States from breaking apart than to see the country divide into two because he allowed the Constitution to get in the way of winning the war.[4]

Troops in battle in Vietnam. During the Vietnam War, Congress tried to repeal a resolution that had allowed President Lyndon Johnson to send a half million troops to Southeast Asia. Newly elected President Richard Nixon claimed he had the authority to keep the troops there anyway.

★ The Commander in Chief Since 1950

A further expansion of the president's power as commander in chief occurred at the start of the Korean War. When South Korea was invaded by North Korea in 1950, President Harry S Truman decided to use military force to defend the country. Truman did this without first seeking congressional approval. Instead, he said that, as commander in chief, he already had the power to do so. The president also argued that the United Nations Security Council resolution that called on all UN members, including the United States, to give military assistance to South Korea was all the authorization that he needed to act.[5]

A decade later, President John F. Kennedy blockaded Cuba without congressional approval during the Cuban Missile Crisis. He also sent sixteen thousand troops to Vietnam as advisers to help the South Vietnamese government fight against North Vietnam and the Vietcong guerrillas without consulting Congress.

In 1964, North Vietnamese patrol boats attacked an American destroyer in the Gulf of Tonkin. In response, Congress passed a resolution allowing President Lyndon B. Johnson to use military force to defend South Vietnam against North Vietnam and the Vietcong. That is when Johnson started to send more than five hundred thousand troops to fight in Vietnam. But when Congress repealed the resolution in 1971, President Richard Nixon claimed that his powers as commander in chief gave him all the authority he needed to continue the Vietnam War.[6]

★ Expansion of Wartime Powers

There have been times when Congress expanded the president's wartime powers. During World War I, Congress gave President Woodrow Wilson the power to control the production and use of the country's industry and natural resources in order to win the war. One statute even allowed him to take steps to conserve America's food supply. Many of these laws only stated broad goals and left it up to Wilson to decide how those goals would be met. Therefore, the president took it upon himself to seize industrial plants and to impose censorship when he deemed it necessary for the war effort.[7]

Of all the presidents, Franklin D. Roosevelt probably made the greatest claim to presidential wartime powers. During World War II, Congress gave Roosevelt many powers similar to what it had given to President Wilson. However, Congress was hesitant in 1942 about repealing a law that the president thought threatened the economy and, thus, the war effort. That led Roosevelt to claim that, as commander in chief, he could repeal by himself any law in wartime that he felt got in the way of victory. This statement alarmed some people in government, but the American public strongly supported him. In the end, rather than confront the president, Congress repealed the law that he opposed.[8]

After America withdrew from the war in Vietnam, many believed that Congress had given away too many of its wartime powers to the president. Congress made an attempt in 1973 to regain some of those powers by passing the War Powers Resolution. Among other things, the law requires the president to withdraw American forces from a military conflict within sixty days (or, in some cases, ninety days) unless Congress declares war or otherwise approves an extended military commitment. President Nixon vetoed the resolution, claiming that it was an unconstitutional restraint on his powers as commander in chief. His veto was overturned by large margins in both the House and Senate. However, most presidents since Nixon have argued that the resolution violates the Constitution.[9]

★ In the Heat of Battle

There have only been two occasions when a president has actually faced enemy fire. During the Civil War, when much of the fighting was near Washington, D.C., President Lincoln visited Fort Stevens in 1864 while it was under attack. Lincoln, however, only watched the battle from behind the walls of the fort. The only president to personally exercise his power as commander in chief in battle was James Madison. On August 19, 1814, during the War of 1812, a British invasion force landed at Benedict, Maryland. The British approached the capital of Washington, D.C., which was only forty miles away. On August 24, the British won a battle at Bladensburg, Maryland. Madison was on the battlefield and, at one point, risking death and capture, he took command of a naval battery in an unsuccessful attempt to prevent the British occupation of Washington.[10]

Artist Allyn Cox painted this mural of his impression of what the scene may have looked like when British troops burned Washington, D.C. President James Madison risked death on the battlefield during the invasion.

During the Civil War, President Lincoln frequently issued direct orders to his generals regarding troop movements. Before the 1940s, however, most other presidents tended to delegate the decisions regarding strategy and tactics to the generals and admirals in the field. But with the invention of nuclear weapons, any mistake in the battlefield can now lead to nuclear war. Furthermore, it currently takes only seconds, instead of weeks and months, to send messages around the world. As a result, most modern presidents have been personally involved in ordering and overseeing even the smallest U.S. military operations across the globe.[11]

★ The President as a Diplomat

Closely related to the president's war powers is his role as America's chief diplomat and the maker of U.S. foreign policy.

The Founding Fathers divided the power to conduct foreign policy between the president and Congress. This was done to prevent the president from entering into alliances and making other international commitments on his own on behalf of the United States. For example, the president can negotiate and sign treaties, but a two-thirds vote in the Senate is needed to ratify the treaty. Likewise, if the treaties require the spending of any government money, then both the House of Representatives and the Senate have to approve the amount spent. The president can also appoint ambassadors to represent the United States around the world, but the Senate must approve those appointments. The power to regulate commerce with foreign nations was given to Congress. Indeed, the only thing mentioned in the Constitution that the president can do himself regarding foreign affairs is to receive ambassadors and other diplomats from other countries.[12]

★ Early Presidents and Diplomacy

A debate soon arose about whether the president or Congress should take the lead in determining foreign policy. In 1793, a war broke out between France and Great Britain. President George Washington made a proclamation declaring that it was America's intent not to take sides in the conflict. Many people denounced the president's action. They argued that because the power to declare war rests only with Congress, then only Congress could determine whether the United States should remain at peace. Therefore, they argued that Washington exceeded his authority when he announced America's neutrality. Washington's supporters, however, believed that the Constitution gives the president very broad and undefined powers with which to conduct foreign affairs. In other words, unless the Constitution specifically states that the president cannot do something, then he can.[13]

Until the 1850s, most presidents took the lead in determining America's foreign policy. For example, President Monroe declared in 1823 that it was official U.S. policy that no European power would be allowed to establish new colonies in the Western Hemisphere or to interfere with the newly independent countries of Latin America. This was called the Monroe Doctrine. He did this on his own initiative. However, there were also times when Congress would not go along with the presidents' policies or took the lead itself. For instance, when relations between the United States and Great Britain worsened in the early 1810s, it was Congress who demanded war while President Madison hesitated. Eventually, Madison caved in and asked Congress for a declaration of war in 1812.[14]

During the last half of the nineteenth century, the presidents took less, and Congress took more, of a leadership role in determining foreign policy. This was because domestic issues, such as slavery, the Civil War, and the reunification of the United States after the war, took most of the presidents' time.

★ Presidents as Diplomats Since 1900

The first modern president to dominate the control of foreign policy was Theodore Roosevelt. Often, Roosevelt would bully, ignore, or work around Congress in matters regarding foreign affairs. For example, in 1907, he wanted to send the American Great White Fleet of battleships on a world cruise to impress other countries with the United States' new, modern navy. At first, Congress refused to fund the voyage but backed down when Roosevelt pointed out that he already had enough money to send the fleet halfway around the world and that it was up to Congress to decide whether the ships would get home.

President Wilson's attempts to ignore Congress in foreign-policy matters were not so successful. After World War I, leaders from around the world, including Wilson, were at Versailles, France, in 1919 to negotiate a peace treaty. At Wilson's insistence, the treaty contained provisions for the creation of an international organization called the League of Nations that was designed to prevent future wars. But Wilson totally ignored Congress; he did not even tell it what he was doing at the conference. So when Wilson

President Woodrow Wilson was disappointed when his efforts to get the United States to join the League of Nations were crushed by the senators who had rejected the Treaty of Versailles that ended World War I. The League of Nations was eventually replaced by the United Nations.

signed the Treaty of Versailles and brought it to the Senate for ratification. Wilson hoped for prompt Senate approval, but feared trouble from Republicans, newly restored as the Senate's majority party. The Senate rejected the agreement and kept the United States out of the league.[15]

The presidents resumed their dominance in foreign policy matters during World War II. There was a need to determine and to coordinate war plans with America's allies to defeat Germany, Italy, and Japan. Likewise, since the end of the war, the United States has been, militarily and economically, the most powerful nation in the world. As a result, America now has interests all around the globe. Dangers, such as international terrorism, have threatened peace and American interests around the world since the 1990s. Nuclear war has been possible ever since the invention of atomic weapons in 1945. All these factors point to the need for America's foreign policy to be handled by a single individual rather than by a large group, such as Congress.

★ Congress's Role in Foreign Affairs

The president does not determine foreign policy alone. Congress still has many powers regarding the conduct of America's relations with other countries and, since the 1970s, has often used them contrary to the president's wishes. One of those powers is the right to determine how the government's money may, and may not, be spent. For instance, Congress passed a law in 1973 that prohibited President Nixon from spending money for military operations in Cambodia and Laos. Nixon had argued that the ability to send troops and planes into those countries might be needed to defend South Vietnam from North Vietnam and the Vietcong.[16]

★ Treaties

One way that the president conducts foreign policy is by using treaties. The Constitution gives the president the power to make treaties with other countries "with the Advice and Consent of the Senate." Opinions about what this phrase means has changed over the years. President Washington once thought that he was personally required to appear before senators to seek their opinions before he could nego- tiate a treaty. So, in 1789, he went to the Senate to discuss a possible treaty with the Creek Indians. The meeting was a chaotic mess, and neither Washington nor any other presi- dent has gone to the Senate for that purpose again. Other presidents, however, have written to the Senate to seek its advice before and during treaty negotiations. Influential senators have also been personally consulted. And some presidents have personally gone to the Senate to seek its approval of a treaty that has already been signed.[17]

The Senate will sometimes make changes to a treaty that has already been signed by the President. This first happened in 1795, when the Senate approved a treaty with Great Britain (called "Jay's Treaty"). The treaty dealt with the with- drawal of British outposts from American soil and the rights of American merchant vessels on the high seas. After much debate, the Senate threw out a provision in the treaty that concerned trade between the United States and the British West Indies.[18]

★ Executive Agreements

Executive agreements are similar to treaties. They are made by the president with the leader or government of another country. Executive agreements are not mentioned in the Constitution. Unlike a treaty, which the Constitution says is the supreme law of the land, an executive agreement cannot override any laws passed by Congress, but it is legally binding so long as it does not violate any such laws. Executive agreements do not need the Senate's ratification, but presidents often seek congressional approval once they are signed. There are no specific rules as to when an executive agreement, rather than a treaty, can be used. Executive agreements are sometimes used when there is a need for speed or secrecy (such

President George Washington sent Chief Justice John Jay (shown here) to help negotiate a treaty with Great Britain. The treaty, which the U.S. Senate made changes to, became known as Jay's Treaty.

as an agreement with another country during wartime). Other times, executive agreements are merely the extension of already existing treaties or a way to implement some law passed by Congress. And, at times, presidents use executive agreements when they wish to reach an agreement with another country but know that it will not get the two-thirds vote needed in the Senate for treaty ratification.

For example, President Franklin D. Roosevelt wanted to give fifty old destroyers to Great Britain in 1940 to help the British fight the Germans in World War II. At that point, the United States had not yet entered the war. Roosevelt knew that he could not get two thirds of the Senate to approve the deal, so he gave the destroyers to the British by signing an executive agreement with the British government. The use of executive agreements has tremendously grown throughout the years. Less than one third of all international agreements that the United States was a party to in 1840 were executive agreements, but, today, it is over 95 percent.[19]

★ Diplomats

The president has the power, subject to the Senate's approval, to appoint ambassadors and other representatives to foreign governments. Many presidents have also appointed personal representatives to carry out specific, but temporary, diplomatic assignments. Because the appointment of these special diplomats does not require Senate confirmation, they are used whenever the president does not wish to involve Congress in a matter regarding foreign policy or when he wishes to convey a personal message to the leaders of another nation. For example, during World War II, President Franklin D. Roosevelt would often send his personal aide, Harry Hopkins, to London and Moscow with messages for the leaders of our allies during the war, Great Britain and the Soviet Union.

During the last hundred years, the president himself has become America's top diplomat. No president before 1906 ever left the United States during his term in office. That year, Theodore Roosevelt went to Central America for a short trip to see how the construction of the Panama Canal was going. Today, presidents frequently leave the country to visit foreign leaders and to conduct diplomatic talks.[20]

★ The Vice President: Role and Responsibilities

The vice president is the president of the Senate, which means that he presides over the senators' debates and deliberations. In the early days when the Senate was small, the vice president was able to direct legislative debates, appoint members to committees, and have some influence on its agenda. However, his powers today are mostly ceremonial. For example, Vice President Walter Mondale spent only about eighteen hours a year carrying out his duties as president of the Senate between 1977 and 1981.

The vice president's most important duty as president of the Senate is to vote whenever there is a tie. Because the Senate is now larger than it once was (it now has one hundred members), the need for the vice president to serve as a tiebreaker has become less frequent. But the vice president can still play an important role in the Senate. In 2001, the Senate was evenly divided between Democrats and Republicans and Vice President Richard Cheney's tie-breaking vote swung control of the Senate in favor of the Republicans.[21]

The vice president's second responsibility is to assume the presidency whenever the president dies, resigns, is removed from office, or is unable to serve due to illness or injury. Only nine times in American history has a vice president become president due to the death or resignation of the president. (No president has ever been removed from office.) The vice president also temporarily assumes the duties of the president whenever the president becomes very sick or is unable to do his work. There have been only a few times when the vice president has temporarily assumed the powers of the president due to the president's inability to do his job. For instance, when President Ronald Reagan went to a hospital for cancer surgery for a few hours in 1985, he handed over the powers and duties of his office to Vice President George H. W. Bush.[22]

The vice president's primary job today is to serve as an adviser to the president and to lead special groups when asked to do so by the president. However, this was not always the case. For most of the 1800s and the early 1900s, whenever there was a presidential election, political parties selected their vice-presidential candidates in order to provide regional or political balance and to increase the party's chances of winning the election. For example, if a party's presidential nominee was from the North, then its candidate for vice president would probably be from the South. If the presidential nominee was a liberal, then the party would probably select a moderate or a conservative as his running mate. The result was that the president and vice president often did not know each other very well, if at all, until after they were elected. Occasionally, they did not even like each other, and sometimes a vice president has publicly opposed the policies and decisions of the president. Therefore, most presidents did not seek their vice president's advice or give them anything to do. For instance, Richard Johnson had so little to do while he was vice president from 1837 to 1841 that he spent most of his time running a tavern in his home state of Kentucky. Since 1940, however, the presidential candidates themselves, instead of the leaders of the political

Modern vice presidents often play a greater role than those vice presidents of long ago. President Barack Obama often consults Vice President Joseph Biden on important policy decisions. President Obama, flanked by Vice President Biden, addresses soldiers with the 101st Airborne Division during a visit to Fort Campbell, Kentucky, on May 6, 2011.

parties, have selected the vice-presidential candidates. The major consequence of this change has been that the vice president is now typically someone whom the president has confidence and trust in.[23]

★ The Vice President Today

Presidents now often benefit from their vice presidents' knowledge and expertise. For example, President Gerald Ford regularly sought the advice of his vice president, Nelson Rockefeller, a former governor of New York, on matters of domestic policy. More recently, President George W. Bush asked for Vice President Cheney's advice on virtually every important decision that he had to make, just as President Bill Clinton did before him with Vice President Al Gore.

Vice presidents are now also asked to chair special presidential commissions. These are often created to look at problems or to implement policies that the president supports. For instance, Vice President Dan Quayle was the chair of the White House Council on Competitiveness, and Vice President Gore chaired the National Performance Review Commission. Both were important bodies that affected how the federal government works.

Recent vice presidents have often worked as liaisons between the president and Congress, passing information and ideas back and forth. They work to obtain congressional support for any new laws or policies that the president wishes to implement.

Vice presidents are also sometimes sent overseas to carry important messages to the leaders of other countries. And vice presidents make speeches across the United States and around the world to improve America's image and to defend the policies and actions of the president.[24]

★ The White House Staff

The president has many things to do. For example, presidents must write letters and give speeches, draft legislative proposals, deal with representatives and other officials, appoint people to various jobs, read hundreds of pages of documents, meet thousands of people, and answer questions from newspaper and television reporters. It is impossible for any single person to do all this. Therefore, the White House Office, which consists of the president's staff and closest advisers, has been created to help the president with these tasks.

The earliest presidents had little or no staff, and what help there was were clerks, secretaries, and typists. So, for example, if the president had to give a speech, he first had to write it himself. Furthermore, Congress provided no funding for any presidential staff until 1857; before then, the president had to pay out of his own pocket anyone he hired to help with the day-to-day functions of his office.

Those early assistants were frequently relatives or close friends of the president. For instance, President Washington hired his nephew to assist him. And so long as the financial resources to pay a staff and the responsibilities of the federal government were small, the White House staff remained small too. By 1933, the size of the president's staff had increased to only four along with about forty clerks and typists.[25]

Many presidents found this situation to be inadequate. Therefore, some presidents borrowed staff from the various departments of the government. Others gave their close advisers jobs within the government so that they would be available whenever the president wanted their advice and help. For example, Amos Kendall was technically the fourth auditor of the treasury, However, he rarely worked

Dan Quayle served as vice president in the administration of President George H. W. Bush. In this photo, Quayle is shaking hands with President Ronald Reagan at a time when Quayle was a senator.

at the Treasury Department. Instead, he spent most of his time at the White House as an unofficial and unpaid adviser and speechwriter for President Andrew Jackson.[26]

★ Expansion of the President's Staff

By 1936, the situation was woefully inadequate, so President Franklin D. Roosevelt created a presidential commission to look into the president's staffing needs. Congress accepted the commission's recommendations in 1939, and Roosevelt was allowed to hire up to six new administrative assistants. Roosevelt eventually had twelve aides as well as sixty-five secretaries and other full-time employees at the White House.[27]

As the size and responsibilities of the federal government grew with each successive president, the size of the White House staff grew as well. In 2001, there were 462 full-time employees at the White House. This included the president's many advisers as well as the clerical staff and the people who help answer questions from the media, meet with congressional representatives and senators, and write speeches. If you count the many interns, volunteers, and people who are borrowed from the various government departments to work at the White House, as well as everyone else who is hired to meet the personal needs of the president (the cooks, limousine drivers, maids, and so on), the number is actually closer to six thousand.[28]

★ The Cabinet and the Executive Departments

The president's Cabinet is a group of advisers who also happen to hold important jobs within the federal government. Neither the Constitution nor any federal law provides for it.

The Constitution permits the president to require the written opinion of the "principal Officer in each of the executive Departments, upon any Subject, relating to the Duties of their respective Offices." This clearly implies a division of the executive branch's administrative work with the president as the person responsible for oversight. It does not, however, formally establish a council of advisers. Indeed, if anybody was to fill such a role, most people alive in Washington's time assumed that the Senate would serve that purpose.[29]

President Andrew Jackson was known for hiring his friends and close advisers. His inner circle was known as the "Kitchen Cabinet."

President Washington informally created the Cabinet. In 1789, he called together the leaders, or "secretaries," of the first three major departments of the federal government (state, war, and the treasury) and the attorney general (who did not yet head a government department) for advice about a possible tour of the United States. The group occasionally met with Washington in 1791 and 1792 to discuss various issues. Then a war between Great Britain and France in 1793 presented America with a foreign policy crisis. Washington started to meet with the Cabinet virtually every day. He also sought each Cabinet member's advice, not only on the matters concerning their executive departments but also on whatever the president wished to discuss. Not all presidents, though, followed this practice. The last president to hold regular Cabinet meetings in order to listen to the advice of all of its members at the same time was Dwight D. Eisenhower. Many presidents rarely met with the entire Cabinet all at once. Some preferred to work closely only with the heads of those departments that were important to pursuing their policies and goals. Others viewed the Cabinet as nothing but a group of administrators and never consulted them at all.[30]

★ The Federal Departments

The Cabinet consists of the heads of the fifteen federal departments. Each department administers the government's programs and implements its policies in specific areas of concern.

The title of each department indicates what topics it deals with. The fifteen are the departments of agriculture, commerce, defense, education, energy, health and human resources, homeland security, housing and urban development, interior (which deals with the conservation of the nation's parks and natural resources), justice, labor, state (which handles America's foreign affairs), transportation, treasury (which manages the country's finances), and veterans affairs. Except for the attorney general, who heads the Department of Justice, all the heads of the federal departments have the title of "secretary." For instance, the secretary of agriculture is the head of the Department of Agriculture.[31]

Under President George W. Bush, six other officials also had Cabinet rank: the vice president, the White House chief of staff, the administrator of the Environmental Protection Agency, the director of the Office of Management and Budget, the director of the National Drug Control Policy, and the U.S. trade representative. At various times, other federal officials have been given Cabinet rank. For example, the U.S. ambassador to the United Nations once had Cabinet rank.[32]

President Washington originally named as department heads the best talent that he could find without regard to political ideology. However, the practice soon arose that a person's loyalty to the president's policies as well as his or her ability is considered when he or she is appointed to lead one of the federal departments.

★ Relying on the Cabinet

Presidents have frequently made important decisions without first consulting their Cabinets. There have also been times when presidents have depended on individual Cabinet members for advice on matters that had nothing to do with the business of that official's department. For example, President Kennedy's attorney general, Robert Kennedy, played a key role in the resolution of the Cuban Missile Crisis, which was an international affair and not a domestic legal matter.

Many presidents have sought the advice of people who were not members of the Cabinet. The best-known example is President Jackson's "Kitchen Cabinet." This group consisted of Jackson's closest friends, some of whom had no job of any kind in the executive branch of government. They included Jackson's private secretary, a former Cabinet member, two newspaper editors, a U.S. senator, and an old army buddy.[33]

★ Independent Government Agencies

In addition to the White House staff and the Cabinet, there are a number of independent government agencies that support the president in his work.

There are four types. Some perform duties similar to an executive department and administer specific government programs. Other agencies look after the interests of particular groups (such as helping the president develop a national strategy to protect consumers or to combat illegal drug use). A third group (such as the National Security Council) helps the president determine government policy. The rest (such as the Office of Management and Budget) perform various management duties.

Congress created many of these agencies while the president himself established the others. There have been more than fifty such agencies since the first one was created in 1921. Today, there are about a dozen in operation.[34]

Among the best known and most important of these supporting agencies are the National Security Council (NSC) and the Office of Management and Budget (the OMB).

Attorney General Robert Kennedy (center) chats with FBI chief J. Edgar Hoover. President John F. Kennedy often asked for his brother's advice on matters unrelated to his job description as attorney general.

★ National Security Council

The NSC was created to advise the president on national security issues. It consists of the president, the vice president, and the secretaries of state and defense. In addition, the director of the CIA (America's spy and foreign intelligence agency) and the chairman of the Joint Chiefs of Staff (the chiefs are the top generals and admirals in the U.S. military) serve as advisers to the NSC. Most of the NSC's work is actually done by staff who are experts on diplomatic and military issues. The head of the NSC's staff is the president's national security advisers (who is technically known as the assistant to the president for national security affairs).

How much influence the NSC's recommendations have on the president and his decisions is largely based on the personal relationship between the president and his national security advisers. President Truman, for example, rarely used the NSC. In contrast, President Nixon was so close to his national security advisers, Henry Kissinger, that Kissinger and the NSC had more influence on America's foreign policy than the secretary of state and the State Department. Differences of opinion between the NSC staff and the experts at the Department of State have also led to tensions and rivalries between the two groups. Interestingly, Kissinger and two other national security advisers (Colin Powell and Condoleezza Rice) later became secretary of state.[35]

★ Office of Management and Budget

The OMB was created by Congress in 1921 and was originally called the Bureau of the Budget. It was the first agency created for the purpose of helping the president perform his job.

Before the OMB was established, every executive department and independent government agency would decide for itself how much money it needed to fulfill its responsibilities. There was no single person or office that controlled the government's finances or its requests to Congress for funding. Instead, the secretary of the treasury would simply put together the estimates from all the executive departments and independent agencies and then forward them to Congress for its approval.

Since the creation of the OMB, the executive departments and independent agencies can no longer determine for themselves how much money they need to do their jobs. They must now submit budgetary estimates to the OMB, and the OMB decides how much money the departments are going to spend. After making those determinations, the OMB makes its recommendations to the president, who then reviews them and makes whatever changes he wants before submitting the final budget to Congress for its approval.[36]

5

How the President
Is Chosen

Millions of Americans vote every four years to elect a president. However, most people do not realize that they are really not directly choosing the next occupant of the White House. Instead, they are voting for a group of individuals called electors whose job it is to select the country's new chief executive.

This indirect method of electing the president was a result of a compromise at the Constitutional Convention. Some of the Founding Fathers wanted Congress to choose the president, but others felt that this would make the chief executive beholden to the legislature for his job. Others thought that the state governors should pick him. There were those who wanted the president to be directly elected by the people, but many objected because they believed too much democracy could lead to mob rule.

★ The Electoral College

The result was a system where every state would elect as many electors as they have senators and representatives in Congress. For example, every state has two senators. So, if a state has only one congressman in the House of Representatives, then that state would be entitled to three presidential electors. Two senators and one congressman equal three electors.

Together, these electors (along with three from Washington, D.C.) make up the Electoral College, and each elector casts one vote.

The Constitution states that it is up to the state legislatures to decide how their state's electors are chosen. Today, in every state, the electors are nominated by the political parties and are elected by the people. Therefore, when someone casts his or her vote for a presidential candidate, he or she is really voting for a group of electors who have promised to vote for that nominee when the Electoral College meets.[1]

In the first two elections (1789 and 1792), there were not yet any political parties in the United States. George Washington, the hero of the American Revolution, received in both elections one vote from every elector. He is the only president in history to be unanimously elected. But by 1796, the first political parties had been established, the Federalists and the Democratic-Republicans. That year, John Adams, a Federalist, was elected to succeed Washington as president. But Thomas Jefferson, the leader of the Democratic-Republicans, received the second-highest number of votes and became vice president. This is the only time in American history when two opposing candidates from different parties were elected president and vice president.

★ The Twelfth Amendment

In 1800, Jefferson and another Democratic-Republican, Aaron Burr, received an equal number of votes for president. It was originally intended that Burr would be Jefferson's vice president, but when the tie vote was announced, Burr suddenly decided that he wanted to be president. It was left to the House of Representatives to break the tie and to make Jefferson the country's next chief executive. This crisis, and the 1796 election, led to the adoption of the Twelfth Amendment to the Constitution in 1804. This change in the Constitution provides for separate votes for president and vice president. Now, the winning political party's vice-presidential candidate, and not the losing party's presidential nominee, becomes vice president. Furthermore, every vice-presidential nominee is a candidate only for the vice presidency and not for the president's job.[2]

It was predicted by some of the Founding Fathers that the House of Representatives would decide most presidential elections. They were wrong. It has happened only once since 1800. In 1824, there were four presidential candidates, and none of them received a majority of that election's 261 electoral votes. Most people expected the House of Representatives to pick Andrew Jackson, because he had received the most votes (99). Instead, the House chose the second-place finisher, John Quincy Adams, who received only 84 votes.

★ When the Person With the Most Votes Loses

There have also been three times when a person was elected president because he received the majority of electoral votes even though more Americans voted for another candidate. This happens because in every state but Maine and Nebraska, the presidential nominee who receives the most popular votes (the votes cast by average Americans), regardless if he wins by one vote or a million, wins all of that state's electoral votes. (In Maine and Nebraska, whoever wins the most popular votes statewide wins two electoral votes and each candidate wins one electoral vote for every congressional district where he receives the most popular votes.)[3]

Although more people voted for Al Gore (right) than George W. Bush (left) in the 2000 presidential election, Bush won the presidency because he received more votes from the Electoral College.

For example, imagine an election where the electoral and popular vote in forty-eight states is a tie. In the forty-ninth state, Candidate A wins a thousand more popular votes than Candidate B and wins all five of that state's electoral votes. But in the fiftieth state, Candidate B wins only ten more popular votes than Candidate A, but as a result he wins all of that state's six electoral votes. In this scenario, Candidate B becomes president because he has one more electoral vote than Candidate A even though Candidate A had 990 more popular votes than Candidate B.[4]

The first time that a nominee was elected president although the other candidate received more popular votes was in 1876. That year, Rutherford B. Hayes defeated Samuel Tilden by winning 185 electoral votes to Tilden's 184, even though Tilden received more than 250,000 more popular votes than Hayes. The second time was in 1888, when Grover Cleveland won more than 90,000 more popular votes than Benjamin Harrison but received only 168 electoral votes to Harrison's 233. And the third time was in 2000, when George W. Bush defeated Al Gore with 271 electoral votes to Gore's 266, although Gore received more than 500,000 more popular votes than Bush.[5]

There have also been a number of times when the switch of a few popular votes in one or more key states would have given victory to the loser. For example, Woodrow Wilson won 600,000 more votes nationwide in 1916 than Charles Evans Hughes. The vote in the Electoral College, however, was quite close (Wilson, 277; Hughes, 254). And in California, Wilson's margin of victory was only about four thousand votes. Had two thousand people in that state voted for Hughes instead of Wilson, California's thirteen electoral votes, and the White House, would have gone to Hughes.[6]

6

How a
President Is Removed
From Office

The Constitution provides that the president shall serve a four-year term. However, it also has provisions for the president's removal from office in case he breaks the law.

The delegates at the Constitutional Convention had many different ideas about why the president might be removed and how to do it. They agreed that the president should lose his office if he committed a serious crime. Some felt that he should be removed if he neglected his job or performed his duties in a negligent way. Others thought that he should be removed if he was inept or dishonest in his work. But many felt that these reasons were too broad and would allow the president to be removed merely because he and the Congress disagreed over politics. The more stringent phrase "treason, bribery, and corruption" was suggested, but even that was too broad for some. The Founding Fathers finally settled on an old saying from British law, "treason, bribery, and other High Crimes and Misdemeanors." The last term in that phrase was understood by all to include major abuses of official power.

★ Impeachment

The Constitutional Convention also had to decide how the president could be removed. Everyone felt that the House of Representatives was the body to impeach or to accuse the president of wrongdoing, but there was disagreement as to who should determine guilt. One group favored the Supreme Court, while another suggested a special court consisting of the highest judges from every state supreme court. It was felt by many that the job should not go to the Senate, because that would make the president too dependent on Congress's goodwill to remain in office. A compromise was reached. The House of Representatives was given the power to impeach the president by a majority vote. However, if the president were impeached, then a trial would be held in the Senate. A two-thirds vote would be needed to convict, making it difficult to remove the country's chief executive for only political purposes.[1]

Only four presidents have ever faced the possibility of impeachment. The first was President John Tyler. During the early 1840s, Tyler and Congress were in a bitter dispute over the creation of a national bank. Tyler believed that to establish such a bank would violate the Constitution, so he vetoed two bills passed by Congress to create one. Tyler also rejected many other pieces of legislation that he thought were unconstitutional, and he became known to his enemies as "Old Veto." One member of the House of Representatives finally got so frustrated with the president that he introduced on January 10, 1843, a resolution calling for Tyler's impeachment. The nine charges listed in the resolution were petty and politically motivated, and the resolution was defeated in the House by a vote of 83 to 127.[2]

THE LAST SPEECH ON IMPEACHMENT—THADDEUS STEVENS

Artist Theodore R. Davis created this engraving depicting Senator Thaddeus Stevens making the final speech before the first vote during President Andrew Johnson's impeachment trial.

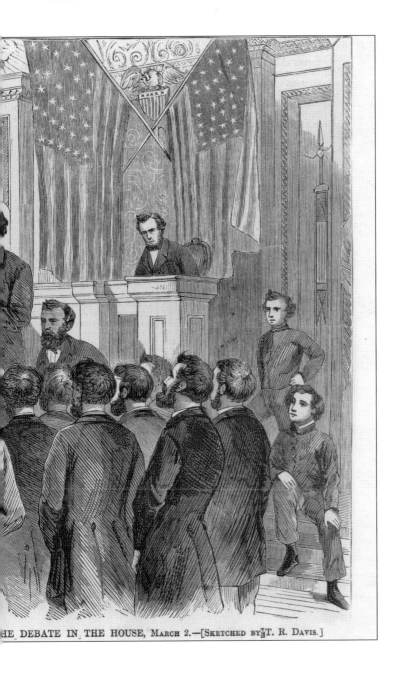

HE DEBATE IN THE HOUSE, March 2.—[Sketched by T. R. Davis.]

★ Johnson and the Tenure of Office Act

The second president to face the threat of impeachment was Andrew Johnson. The immediate cause of Johnson's impeachment was his firing of Secretary of War Edwin Stanton. The Tenure of Office Act, which was adopted in 1867 over Johnson's veto, prohibited the president from removing any government official without the Senate's approval if that person's original appointment required Senate confirmation. President Abraham Lincoln named Stanton secretary of war in 1862, and the Senate confirmed the appointment. Johnson kept Stanton at his post after Lincoln's death in 1865, but came to suspect that Stanton was secretly helping Johnson's enemies (which he was). In reality, Stanton's firing was the latest event in Johnson's fight with Congress. For three years, he and the legislature strongly disagreed over how to reunite the country after the Civil War. Therefore, like President Tyler, Johnson vetoed many bills that were passed by Congress, leading Johnson's opponents to call him "King Andy the First" and "Sir Veto."

To test the constitutionality of the Tenure of Office Act, Johnson fired Stanton on February 21, 1868. But instead of the matter going to the courts, it gave Congress an excuse to get rid of the president. Three days later, the House of Representatives impeached the president by a vote of 126 to 47 and adopted eleven specific charges a week later. On March 5, a ten-week trial started in the Senate. Johnson was acquitted on May 16 and kept his job, but only by a one-vote margin. With 36 votes needed to meet the two-thirds vote requirement for conviction, the vote was 35 to 19.[3]

★ Nixon and Watergate

Richard Nixon was the third president to face impeachment charges. His troubles began in 1972, when five men were arrested for breaking into the offices of the Democratic Party. (Nixon was a Republican.) Over the next two years, it was revealed that the president agreed to pay money to the burglars in order to keep them from talking about members of the White House staff and Nixon's reelection campaign who were involved in the crime. The president also tried to get the CIA to stop an inquiry by the FBI (America's national police force) into the burglary. Both of these acts constituted a serious criminal offense known as obstruction of justice. In addition, other illegal acts by members of Nixon's Cabinet and staff were revealed, and many of his staff members went to jail. This became known as the Watergate scandal, named after the hotel where the break-in occurred.

On July 27, 1974, the House of Representatives Committee on the Judiciary voted to recommend three articles of impeachment to the full House. (Interestingly, the committee rejected two other articles. One accused the president of abusing his war-making powers by conducting a secret war in Cambodia. The other dealt with Nixon's admission that he illegally evaded paying income taxes. The committee felt that neither of these charges was serious enough to warrant impeachment.) It became clear that Nixon would soon be impeached and convicted, and he resigned his office on August 9.[4]

★ Clinton

The last president to face impeachment was Bill Clinton. In 1994, a woman sued him for sexually harassing her three years earlier while he was governor of Arkansas. As a part of an ongoing investigation arising from that case, it was alleged that the president lied to a grand jury in 1998 about his relationship with another woman, Monica Lewinsky. On December 19, 1998, the House of Representatives passed two articles of impeachment. The first accused the president of lying to the grand jury about Lewinsky and passed by a vote of 228 to 206. The second charged Clinton with obstruction of justice and was approved 221 to 212. Two other articles, one accusing Clinton of perjury at a court hearing involving the sexual harassment case and another charging him with abuse of power, were defeated.

A five-week trial in the Senate began on January 7, 1999. During Clinton's impeachment proceedings and trial, there was much debate whether his alleged lying to a grand jury about a love affair was a serious enough offense to warrant his removal from office. The Senate acquitted Clinton on February 12. On the first charge, there were only 45 votes in favor of a conviction and 55 votes against. On the obstruction of justice charge, the vote was 50 to 50.[5]

7

Running the Country When the President Is Sick

The Founding Fathers gave a lot of thought to how and why a president should be removed by impeachment if he should ever break the law. But little was said in the Constitution about what happens when the president becomes mentally or physically unable to serve.

Article II states that if the president were unable to carry out his duties and powers, then "the Same shall devolve on the Vice President . . . until the Disability is removed, or a President elected." However, nowhere in the Constitution was it mentioned what constitutes a disability or who determines that it exists. This oversight has occasionally presented significant difficulties.

★ Garfield

On July 2, 1881, a madman shot President James Garfield. The president lingered for nearly three months while doctors tried to find and remove the bullet. During this time, Garfield's only official act was to sign one document. But there was no agreement as to what should be done. There were disputes as to whether the "disability" mentioned in the Constitution had to be permanent. There were different

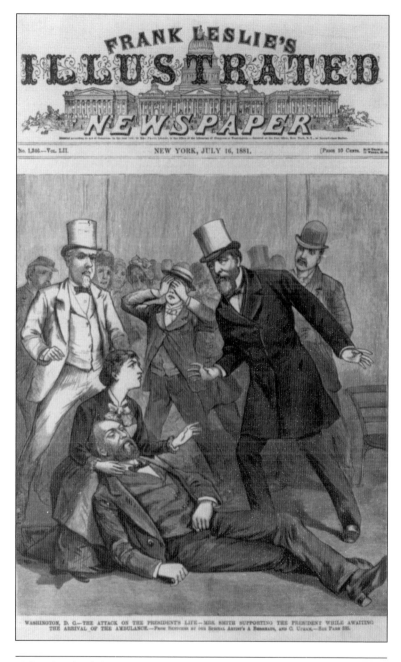

This sketch of the assassination of President James A. Garfield appeared in *Frank Leslie's Illustrated Newspaper* in 1881.

opinions about whether the term applied only to mental disabilities or to physical ones as well. There were also disagreements as to whether it was the vice president or Congress who had the power to declare that a disability existed. Not wanting to appear eager to take over the presidency, Vice President Chester Alan Arthur stayed away from Washington and remained at his home in New York. The federal government, without its leader, virtually came to a halt and little was accomplished. Finally, on September 19, Garfield died, and Arthur became president the next day.[1]

★ Wilson

A similar situation occurred nearly forty years later. On September 26, 1919, President Woodrow Wilson suffered a stroke. Another stroke followed on October 2, and, two days later, he had a complete physical breakdown. The president was bedridden for seven months, and he never fully recovered. During that time, Wilson's wife, Edith, controlled all access to her husband. Although she claimed that his mental abilities were unaffected and that she made no executive decisions of her own, Mrs. Wilson would not permit any person or document to reach the president that she did not want him to see. Edith Wilson also acted as her husband's only spokesperson, and many believed that she was secretly performing some of the president's duties.

Furthermore, President Wilson refused during those seven months to temporarily turn over his duties and powers to Vice President Thomas Marshall. As time passed, people said something should be done, but Marshall was reluctant to appear as if he were trying to seize power. So, just

Woodrow Wilson and wife, Edith Galt Wilson, riding in backseat of a carriage to his second inauguration, March 5, 1917. She has been labeled "the Secret President" and "the first woman to run the government" for the role she played when her husband suffered prolonged and disabling illness after a stroke in October 1919.

as when President Garfield was dying, the operation of the federal government essentially ceased until Wilson recovered enough the following April to resume his duties.[2]

★ Eisenhower

Finally, in the 1950s, President Dwight D. Eisenhower suffered a number of serious ailments that required the president to go to the hospital and to rest before returning to work. The period of time that Eisenhower was unable to work during these illnesses ranged from two days to six weeks. Each time, Vice President Richard Nixon and Presidential Assistant Sherman Adams performed most of the president's duties with his consent. However, every president is also the commander in chief of America's military forces. At the time, the United States was engaged in the Cold War with the Soviet Union. With both sides possessing nuclear weapons, the incapacity of the president, even for a short time, could be disastrous. This caused Eisenhower to worry about what might happen if he had to go to the hospital again. Therefore, Eisenhower and Nixon agreed in 1958 that Nixon would take over the duties and powers of the presidency should Eisenhower ever fall ill again.[3]

★ Kennedy and the Twenty-fifth Amendment

A similar agreement was reached between President John F. Kennedy and Vice President Lyndon B. Johnson when Kennedy became president in 1961. In 1963, Kennedy was murdered, and Johnson became president. There were new concerns, because there was now no vice president to take over should Johnson die or became ill until another one was elected in 1964. That led to the Twenty-fifth Amendment

A somber moment in American history. Lyndon B. Johnson is sworn in as U.S. president hours after President John Kennedy was shot to death. Johnson's wife, Lady Bird, is to the left and Kennedy's widow, Jacqueline, is to the right.

to the Constitution, which was adopted in 1967. That amendment provides detailed procedures that allow the vice president to act as president whenever the chief executive is unable to perform his duties and powers of office. It also allows the president to appoint a new vice president, with Congress's approval, should there ever be a vacancy in the vice presidency.[4]

The provisions of the Twenty-fifth Amendment have rarely been used. When a would-be assassin shot President Ronald Reagan on March 30, 1981, Reagan underwent a two-hour operation that was followed by twelve days of rest before he could return to work. However, even though the president was still awake and alert before he went into surgery, neither he nor anyone else thought to invoke the Twenty-fifth Amendment and to give Reagan's duties and powers to Vice President George H. W. Bush. Four years later, before Reagan had an operation for cancer, he handed over power to Bush for eight hours, but only after protesting that the Twenty-fifth Amendment was not intended to apply for such short periods of time. Finally, when President George W. Bush had an operation in 2002, he temporarily handed over his duties and powers to Vice President Richard Cheney without any objections.[5]

★ Growth and Evolution

The Twenty-fifth Amendment is just the latest step in the growth and evolution of the presidency. When George Washington became the country's first chief executive more than two hundred years ago, his role in the lives of the American people was small. But in modern times, our president makes decisions every day that affect us all. He is the head of a large bureaucracy that protects and benefits Americans, and he plays a major role in the writing of the country's laws. In addition, the president is the country's top law-enforcement officer, diplomat, and military commander. And with the Twenty-fifth Amendment, Americans do not have to worry about whether the federal government will always be working for them, even if the president is not healthy enough to do his job.

Glossary

ambassador—A person sent to another country to represent his or her own country. An official messenger.

bill—A law that has been proposed.

bribery—The act of influencing someone's decision by promising him a favor, money, etc.

delegate—A person who represents a particular group, organization, state, or country at a conference or convention.

dictatorship—A form of government in which total power is controlled by one person.

Electoral College—A group of electors (individuals whose job is to vote in an election) who choose the president and vice president of the United States.

enact—To make a bill into law.

impeach—To charge a public official with crime or misdemeanor.

implement—Put something into practice, such as a law, program, or policy.

impoundment—When a president refuses to spend money that has been allotted to him by Congress.

legislation—The laws made by the legislative branch of a government.

liaison—A person who sets up and keeps a connection between two persons or groups.

override—To overrule or to reject.

pardon—When a person who has been accused or convicted of a crime or offense is pardoned, he or she has been officially and totally forgiven.

quarantine—The enforced isolation of a person or place.

ratify—To legally approve.

repeal—To cancel.

reprieve—The reduction of a sentence or fine given by a court to a convicted criminal.

successor—The person who takes over the position of throne, title, office, or estate of someone else. For example, President Bill Clinton's successor was President George W. Bush.

treason—The giving of aid or comfort to the enemies of one's country or betraying the allegiance or duty of obedience owed to one's government.

treaty—A formal agreement between countries that is made through talk and negotiation.

tyrant—A dictator who uses his or her power cruelly and oppressively. A bully.

veto—To reject or to prevent the passing of a bill.

Chapter Notes

Chapter 1. The Presidency in Action: The Cuban Missile Crisis

1. David L. Larson, ed., *The Cuban Crisis of 1962: Selected Documents, Chronology, and Bibliography,* Second Edition (Lanham, Md.: University Press of America, 1986), p. 10.

2. Arthur M. Schlesinger, Jr., *A Thousand Days: John F. Kennedy in the White House* (Boston: Houghton Mifflin Company, 1965), pp. 179–200, 229–234.

3. Larson, p. 4.

4. Ibid., pp. 6, 12.

5. Schlesinger, pp. 668–674.

6. Ibid., p. 677.

7. Richard Reeves, *President Kennedy: Profile of Power* (New York: Simon and Schuster, 1993), pp. 396–398, 415–416, 418.

8. Ibid., pp. 404–406, 410–413.

9. Schlesinger, pp. 687–691.

10. Reeves, pp. 420–423.

11. Ibid., pp. 423–425.

Chapter 2. Origins of the Presidency

1. Michael Nelson, "The Constitutional Presidency," *The Presidency: A History of the Office of the President of the United States From 1789 to the Present* (London: Salamander Books, Ltd., 1996), p. 9.

2. Edward S. Corwin, Randall W. Bland, Theodore T. Hindson, and Jack W. Peltason, *The President: Office and Powers, 1878–1984,* Fifth Revised Edition (New York: New York University Press, 1984), pp. 6–7.

3. Michael Nelson, "Constitutional Beginnings," *Guide to the Presidency,* Third Edition, Volume I (Washington: CQ Press, 2002), pp. 5–7.

4. Nelson, "The Constitutional Presidency," pp. 9–10, 17–20.

Chapter 3. Duties of the President

1. Edward S. Corwin, Randall W. Bland, Theodore T. Hindson, and Jack W. Peltason, *The President: Office and Powers, 1878–1984,* Fifth Revised Edition (New York: New York University Press, 1984), pp. 85–87.

2. W. Craig Bledsoe, James Brian Watts, and Mark J. Rozell, "Chief Executive," Michael Nelson, ed., *Guide to the Presidency,* Third Edition, Volume I (Washington: CQ Press, 2002), p. 494.

3. Mark E. Byrnes, "The President and the Bureaucracy," Michael Nelson, ed., *Guide to the Presidency,* Third Edition, Volume II (Washington: CQ Press, 2002), pp. 1456–1457.

4. Bledsoe, et al., "Chief Executive," p. 471.

5. Ibid., p. 529.

6. Ibid., pp. 528–529.

7. Ibid., p. 536.

8. In re Neagle, 135 U.S. 1 (1890); In re Debs, 158 U.S. 564 (1895).

9. Joseph Nathan Kane, Janet Podell, and Steven Anzovin, *Facts About the Presidents: A Compilation of Biographical and Historical Information,* Seventh Edition (New York: H. W. Wilson Company, 2001), p. 443.

10. Christopher J. Bosso, "Legislative Leader," Michael Nelson, ed., *Guide to the Presidency,* Third Edition, Volume II (Washington: CQ Press, 2002), p. 571.

11. Sidney M. Milkis, "History of the Presidency," Michael Nelson, ed., *Guide to the Presidency,* Third Edition, Volume I (Washington: CQ Press, 2002), pp. 76, 78–79.

12. Robert J. Spitzer, "The President and Congress," Michael Nelson, ed., *Guide to the Presidency,* Third Edition, Volume II (Washington: CQ Press, 2002), pp. 1351–1356.

13. Kane, et al., p. 669.

14. Bosso, pp. 559–561.

15. Kane, et al., p. 669.

16. Bledsoe, et al., "Chief Executive," pp. 509–510.

17. Ibid., p. 557.

Chapter 4. Foreign Affairs, Vice Presidents, and Official Staff

1. Daniel C. Diller and Stephen H. Wirls, "Commander in Chief," Michael Nelson, ed., *Guide to the Presidency,* Third Edition, Volume I (Washington: CQ Press, 2002), p. 639.

2. Edward S. Corwin, et al., *The President: Office and Powers, 1878–1984,* Fifth Revised Edition (New York: New York University Press, 1984), pp. 228–234.

3. Diller and Wirls, "Commander in Chief," p. 643.

4. Mark Byrnes, "The Civil War Presidents," Michael Nelson, ed., *The Presidency: A History of the Office of the President of the United States From 1789 to the Present* (London: Salamander Books, Ltd., 1996), p. 101.

5. Diller and Wirls, "Commander in Chief," p. 649.

6. Ibid., pp. 650–651.

7. Corwin, et al., pp. 269–270.

8. Ibid., pp. 272–276, 285–286.

9. Ibid., pp. 299–300.

10. Joseph Nathan Kane, Janet Podell, and Steven Anzovin, *Facts About the Presidents: A Compilation of Biographical and Historical Information,* Seventh Edition (New York: H. W. Wilson Company, 2001), pp. 58, 183.

11. Diller and Wirls, "Commander in Chief," pp. 663–665.

12. Corwin, et al., pp. 214–215.

13. Daniel C. Diller and Stephen H. Wirls, "Chief Diplomat," Michael Nelson, ed., *Guide to the Presidency,* Third Edition, Volume I (Washington: CQ Press, 2002), p. 602.

14. Diller and Wirls, "Chief Diplomat," pp. 602–603.

15. Ibid., p. 603.

16. Ibid., p. 606.

17. Christopher J. Bosso, "Legislative Leader," Michael Nelson, ed., *Guide to the Presidency*, Third Edition, Volume I (Washington: CQ Press, 2002), p. 571.

18. Sidney M. Milkis, "History of the Presidency," Michael Nelson, ed., *Guide to the Presidency*, Third Edition, Volume II (Washington: CQ Press, 2002), p. 68.

19. Corwin, et al., pp. 242–246.

20. Diller and Wirls, "Chief Diplomat," pp. 624–627.

21. Michael Nelson, "Office of the Vice President," *Guide to the Presidency*, Third Edition, Volume II (Washington: CQ Press, 2002), pp. 1089–1090.

22. Ibid., pp. 1090–1091.

23. Charles C. Euchner, John Anthony Maltese, and Michael Nelson, "The Electoral Process," Michael Nelson, ed., *Guide to the Presidency*, Third Edition, Volume I (Washington: CQ Press, 2002), p. 271.

24. Nelson, "Office of the Vice President," pp. 1092–1096.

25. Stephen L. Robertson, "The Seat of Presidential Power," Michael Nelson, ed., *The Presidency: A History of the Office of the President of the United States From 1789 to the Present* (London: Salamander Books, Ltd., 1996), p. 53.

26. Robertson, "Executive Office of the President: White House Office," p. 1100.

27. Ibid., pp. 1100–1101.

28. Ibid., pp. 1108–1109.

29. W. Craig Bledsoe and Adriel Bettelheim, "The Cabinet and Executive Departments," Michael Nelson, ed., *Guide to the Presidency*, Third Edition, Volume II (Washington: CQ Press, 2002), p. 1172.

30. Ibid., pp. 1173–1178.

31. "President Bush's Cabinet," *The White House: President George W. Bush,* n.d., <http://www.whitehouse.gov/government/cabinet.html> (April 28, 2007).

32. Ibid.

33. Stephen L. Robertson, "The First Lady, the First Family, and the President's Friends," Michael Nelson, ed., *Guide to the Presidency,* Third Edition, Volume II (Washington: CQ Press, 2002), pp. 1082, 1086.

34. W. Craig Bledsoe and Deborah Kalb, "Executive Office of the Presidents: Supporting Organizations," Michael Nelson, ed., *Guide to the Presidency,* Third Edition, Volume II (Washington: CQ Press, 2002), pp. 1127–1128.

35. Ibid., pp. 1143–1147.

36. John A. Maltese, "The American System," Michael Nelson, ed., *The Presidency: A History of the Office of the President of the United States From 1789 to the Present* (London: Salamander Books, Ltd., 1996), pp. 25–26.

Chapter 5. How the President Is Chosen

1. Michael Nelson, "The Constitutional Presidency," *The Presidency: A History of the Office of the President of the United States From 1789 to the Present* (London: Salamander Books, Ltd., 1996), p. 10.

2. Charles C. Euchner and John L. Moore, "Chronology of Presidential Elections," Michael Nelson, ed., *Guide to the Presidency,* Third Edition, Volume I (Washington: CQ Press, 2002), pp. 323–325.

3. Harold E. Bass, Jr., "Electing the President," Michael Nelson, ed., *The Presidency: A History of the Office of the President of the United States From 1789 to the Present* (London: Salamander Books, Ltd., 1996), pp. 44–45.

4. Charles C. Euchner, John Anthony Maltese, and Michael Nelson, "The Electoral Process," Michael Nelson, ed., *Guide to the Presidency,* Third Edition, Volume I (Washington: CQ Press, 2002), pp. 200, 298.

5. Euchner and Moore, "Chronology of Presidential Elections," pp. 344–345, 348, 393–394.

6. Ibid., p. 355.

Chapter 6. How a President Is Removed From Office

1. Margaret Jane Wyszomirski and Michael Nelson, "Removal of the President," Michael Nelson, ed., *Guide to the Presidency*, Third Edition, Volume I (Washington: CQ Press, 2002), p. 440.

2. Sidney M. Milkis, "History of the Presidency," Michael Nelson, ed., *Guide to the Presidency*, Third Edition, Volume I (Washington: CQ Press, 2002), p. 83.

3. Mark Byrnes, "The Civil War Presidents," Michael Nelson, ed., *The Presidency: A History of the Office of the President of the United States From 1789 to the Present* (London: Salamander Books, Ltd., 1996), pp. 106–107.

4. Burton I. Kaufman, "The Contemporary Presidency," Michael Nelson, ed., *The Presidency: A History of the Office of the President of the United States From 1789 to the Present* (London: Salamander Books, Ltd., 1996), pp. 169–170.

5. Milkis, "History of the Presidency," pp. 169–170.

Chapter 7. Running the Country When the President Is Sick

1. Margaret Jane Wyszomirski and Michael Nelson, "Removal of the President," Michael Nelson, ed., *Guide to the Presidency*, Third Edition, Volume I (Washington: CQ Press, 2002), pp. 433, 457.

2. Stephen L. Robertson, "The First Ladies," Michael Nelson, ed., *The Presidency: A History of the Office of the President of the United States From 1789 to the Present* (London: Salamander Books, Ltd., 1996), p. 193.

3. Wyszomirski and Nelson, "Removal of the President," pp. 458–460.

4. Ibid., p. 460.

5. Ibid., p. 461.

Further Reading

Cheney, Lynne. *We the People: The Story of Our Constitution.* New York: Simon and Schuster, 2008.

Haykim, Joy. *All the People: Since 1945.* New York: Oxford University Press, 2010.

Landau, Elaine. *The President, Vice President, and Cabinet: A Look at the Executive Branch.* New York: Lerner Pub Group, 2012.

Parvis, Sarah. *TIME for Kids President Obama: A Day in the Life of America's Leader.* New York: Time for Kids, 2009.

Sobel, Syl. *The U.S. Constitution and You.* New York: Barron's Educational Series, 2012.

Internet Addresses

The Executive Branch
This Web site is the office site for the White House. It offers in-depth descriptions on the different branches of government, history, fun facts, and other useful resources.
<http://www.whitehouse.gov/our-government/executive-branch>

USA.Gov
The president is the head of the executive branch of the government, which includes many departments and agencies. Explore and learn about these throughout this Web site.
<http://www.usa.gov/Agencies/Federal/Executive.shtml>

Congress for Kids
This Web site offers a unique and fun way to learn about the different branches of government.
<http://www.congressforkids.net/Constitution_threebranches.htm>

THE PRESIDENTS
OF THE UNITED STATES

1789–1797	George Washington
1797–1801	John Adams
1801–1809	Thomas Jefferson
1809–1817	James Madison
1817–1825	James Monroe
1825–1829	John Quincy Adams
1829–1837	Andrew Jackson
1837–1841	Martin Van Buren
March–April, 1841	William Henry Harrison
1841–1845	John Tyler
1845–1849	James K. Polk
1849–1850	Zachary Taylor
1850–1853	Millard Fillmore
1853–1857	Franklin Pierce
1857–1861	James Buchanan
1861–1865	Abraham Lincoln
1865–1869	Andrew Johnson
1869–1877	Ulysses S. Grant
1877–1881	Rutherford B. Hayes
March–Sept., 1881	James A. Garfield
1881–1885	Chester Alan Arthur
1885–1889	Grover Cleveland
1889–1893	Benjamin Harrison
1893–1897	Grover Cleveland
1897–1901	William McKinley
1901–1909	Theodore Roosevelt
1909–1913	William Howard Taft
1913–1921	Woodrow Wilson
1921–1923	Warren G. Harding
1923–1929	Calvin Coolidge
1929–1933	Herbert Hoover
1933–1945	Franklin D. Roosevelt
1945–1953	Harry S Truman
1953–1961	Dwight D. Eisenhower
1961–1963	John F. Kennedy
1963–1969	Lyndon B. Johnson
1969–1974	Richard M. Nixon
1974–1977	Gerald R. Ford
1977–1981	Jimmy Carter
1981–1989	Ronald Reagan
1989–1993	George H. W. Bush
1993–2001	Bill Clinton
2001–2008	George W. Bush
2009–present	Barack Obama

Index